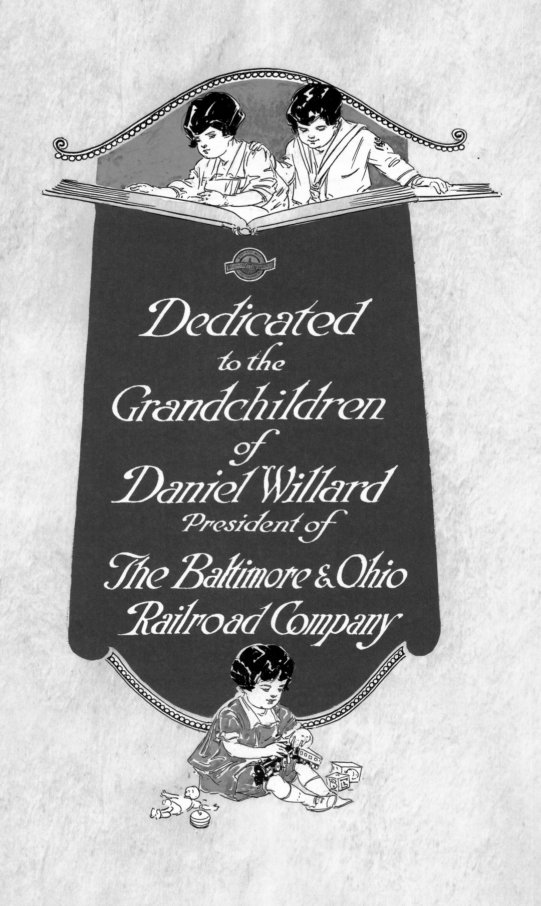

Dedicated
to the
Grandchildren
of
Daniel Willard
President of

The Baltimore & Ohio
Railroad Company

ABC

Choo Choo Book

by Aunt Mary

For the Girl and the Boy
about the Best and Oldest Railroad in the Land.

Distributed by:
United Souvenir & Apparel, Inc.1-800-933-2220
Written by Aunt Mary (Margaret Talbott Stevens)
Illustrated by Uncle Dick (Charles H. Dickson)
Artwork restored by: H.Y. Ting-Bornfreund
©1931 BY BALTIMORE & OHIO RAILROAD COMPANY, BALTIMORE, MD.
©2005 BY THE BALTIMORE & OHIO RAILROAD MUSEUM, INC.
BKRR1 Designed in the USA Printed in China

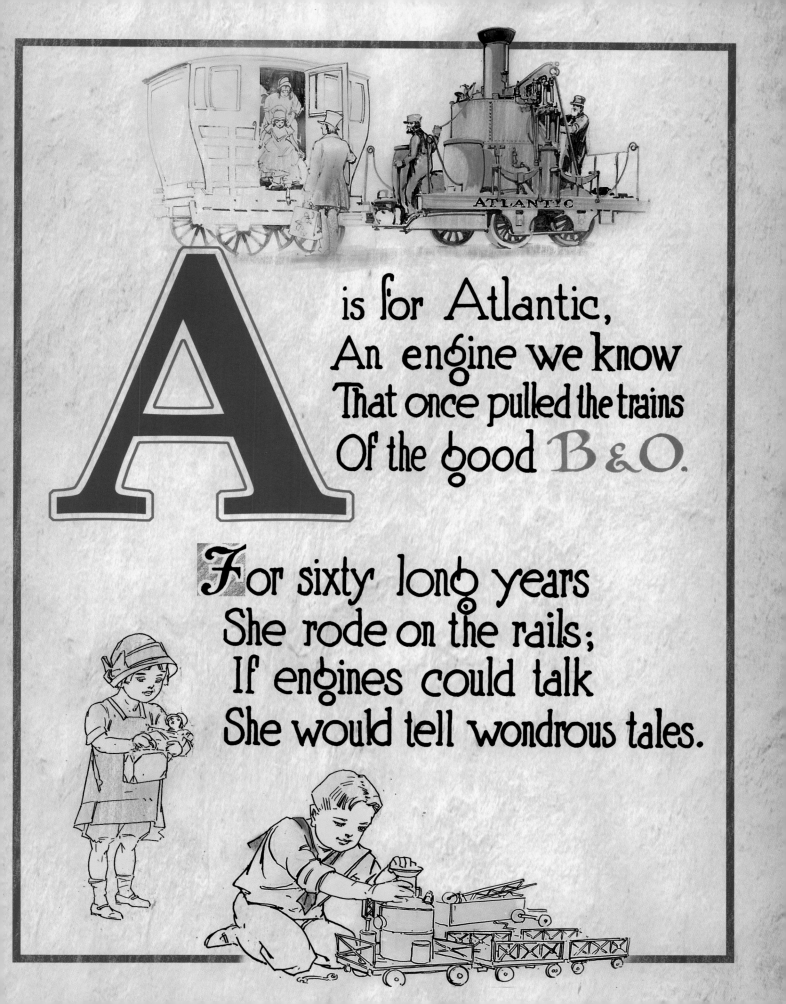

A is for Atlantic,
An engine we know
That once pulled the trains
Of the good B & O.

For sixty long years
She rode on the rails;
If engines could talk
She would tell wondrous tales.

B is for Baltimore,
'Twas here years ago
That our Railroad began
Like an acorn to grow.

And now like the oak-tree,
Sturdy and strong,
It stretches its rails
Seven thousand miles long.

C is for courteous,
As you'll find the crew,
The conductor, the brakeman,
The engineer, too.

The secretary, barber,
The maid, if you choose,
And the smiling old porter
Who brushes your shoes.

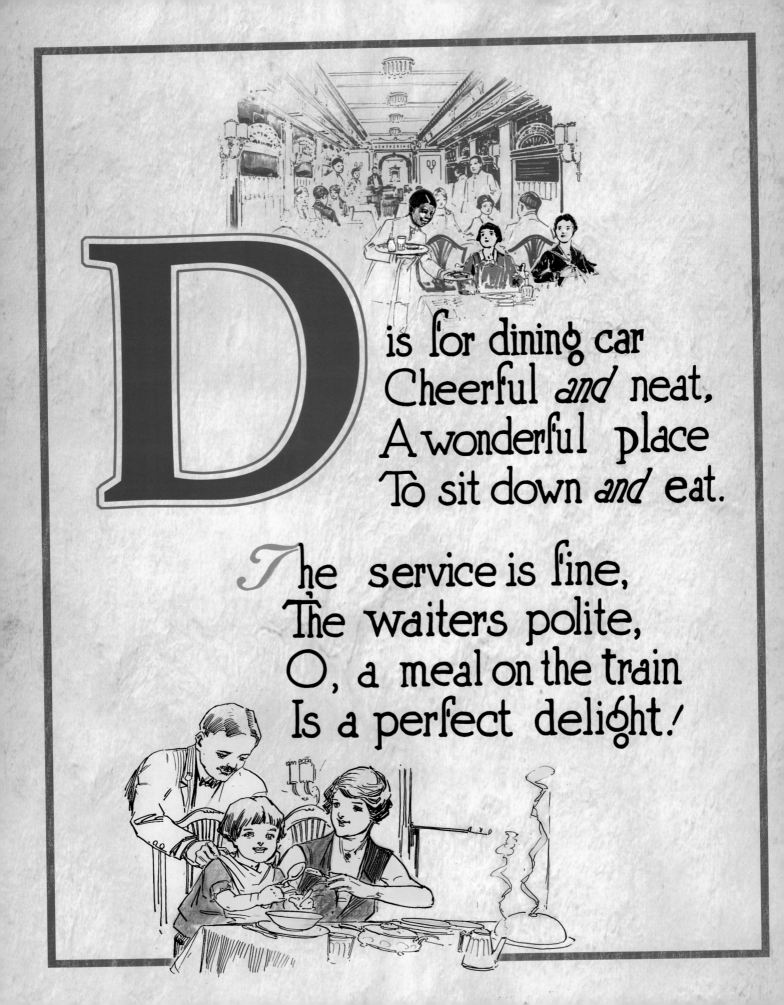

D is for dining car
Cheerful *and* neat,
A wonderful place
To sit down *and* eat.

The service is fine,
The waiters polite,
O, a meal on the train
Is a perfect delight!

E is for engine
That pulls the big train,
We hear its gay whistle
In sunshine *and* rain.

See its long trainloads
Of people or freight;
We tell our time by it
So seldom 'tis late.

F is for freight car,
We'll fill it up high
And invite all our neighbors
This service to try.

For once they have traveled
Or shipped B and O,
They'll know it's the best way
To ship or to go.

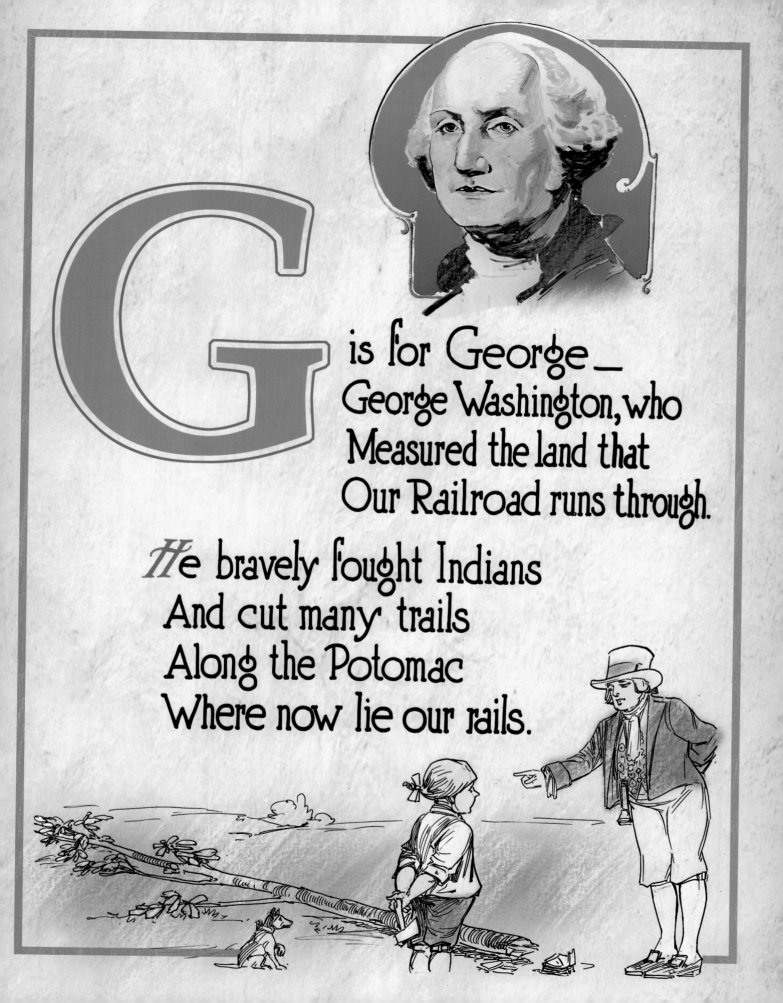

G is for George —
George Washington, who
Measured the land that
Our Railroad runs through.

He bravely fought Indians
And cut many trails
Along the Potomac
Where now lie our rails.

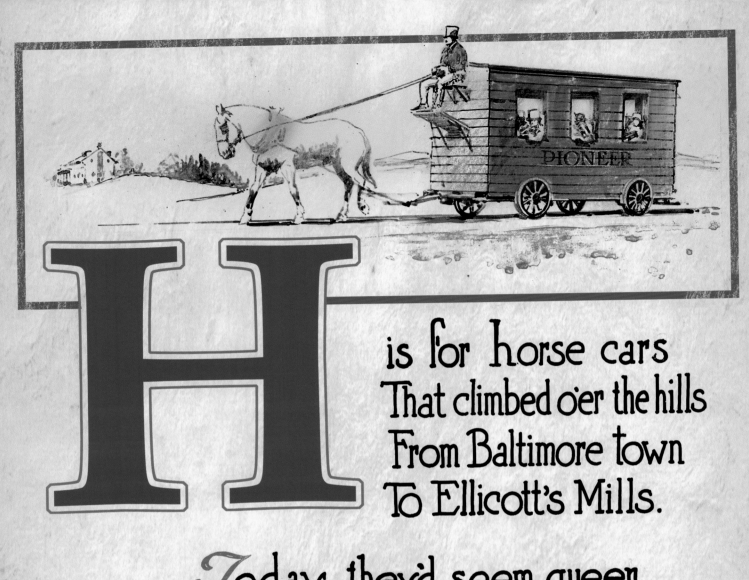

H

is for horse cars
That climbed o'er the hills
From Baltimore town
To Ellicott's Mills.

Today they'd seem queer
And so out of date,
But then all the youngsters
Thought they were great.

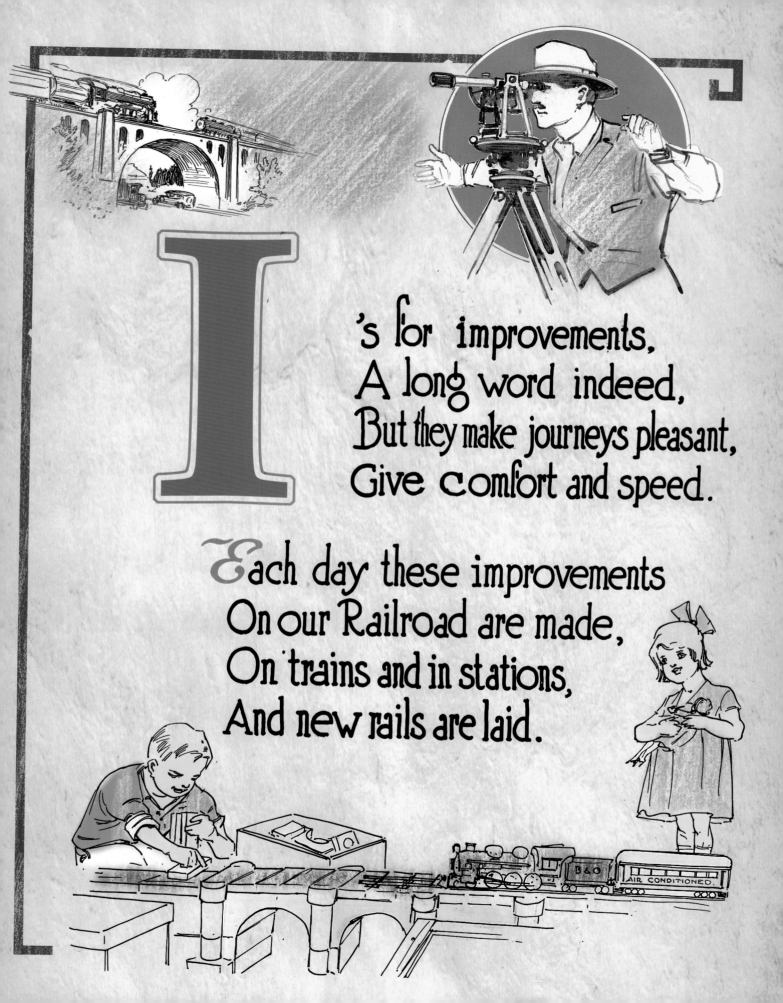

I's for improvements,
A long word indeed,
But they make journeys pleasant,
Give comfort and speed.

Each day these improvements
On our Railroad are made,
On trains and in stations,
And new rails are laid.

J is for Jersey,
The city where we
Get on the big ferry
And *the* skyline we see.

For , like Cinderella,
In motor coach gay,
We're off to New York
Without a delay.

K is for kindness;
The coach-driver sees
That we are well cared for,
He's anxious to please.

And the friendly attendant
Looks well at the tags
And sees that no traveler
Is bothered with bags.

L is for limiteds_
Two of the best,
The Capitol and National
That go east and west.

The Capitol speeds
To Chicago and back,
To St. Louis the National
Flies over the track.

FIRST RELAY

FIRST KEY

FIRST RECEIVER

S.F.B. MORSE

M is for Morse
Who, long, long ago,
Made the first telegraph;
And the good B&O

Received his first message,
All written in "code".
Now thousands are used
All over the Road.

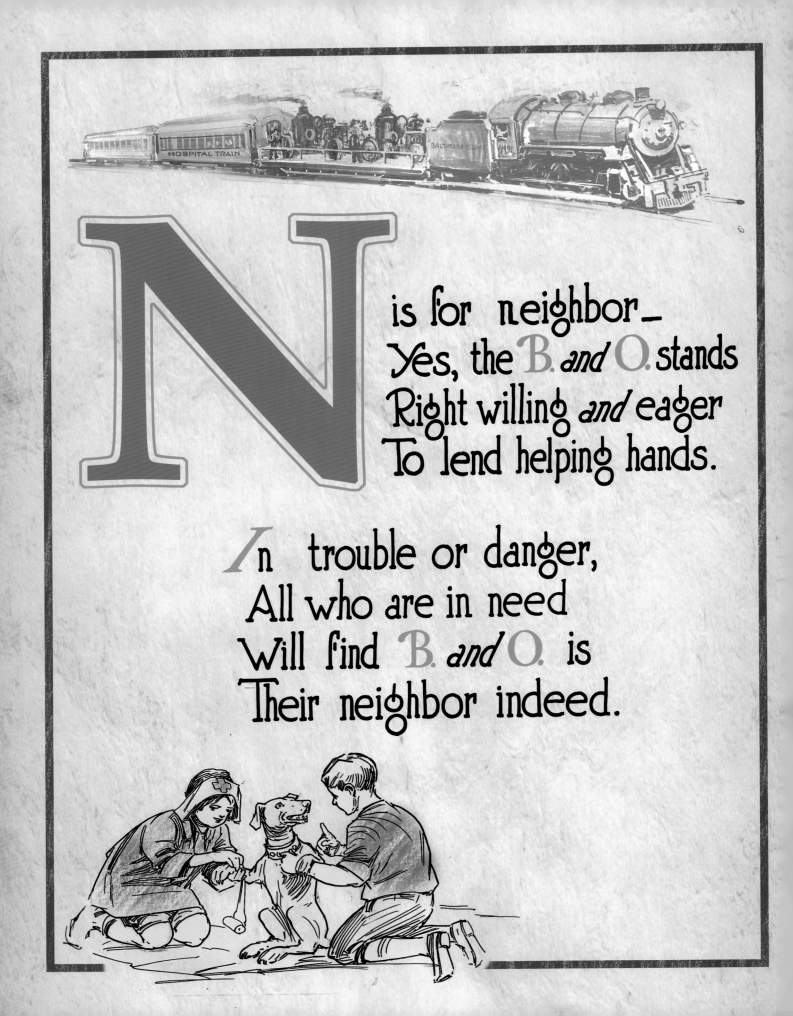

N is for neighbor—
Yes, the B. and O. stands
Right willing and eager
To lend helping hands.

In trouble or danger,
All who are in need
Will find B. and O. is
Their neighbor indeed.

O is for orders
That trainmen receive;
And they do as they're told,
As you may believe.

Each man has his job,
Each job must be done
That our B and O trains
In safety may run.

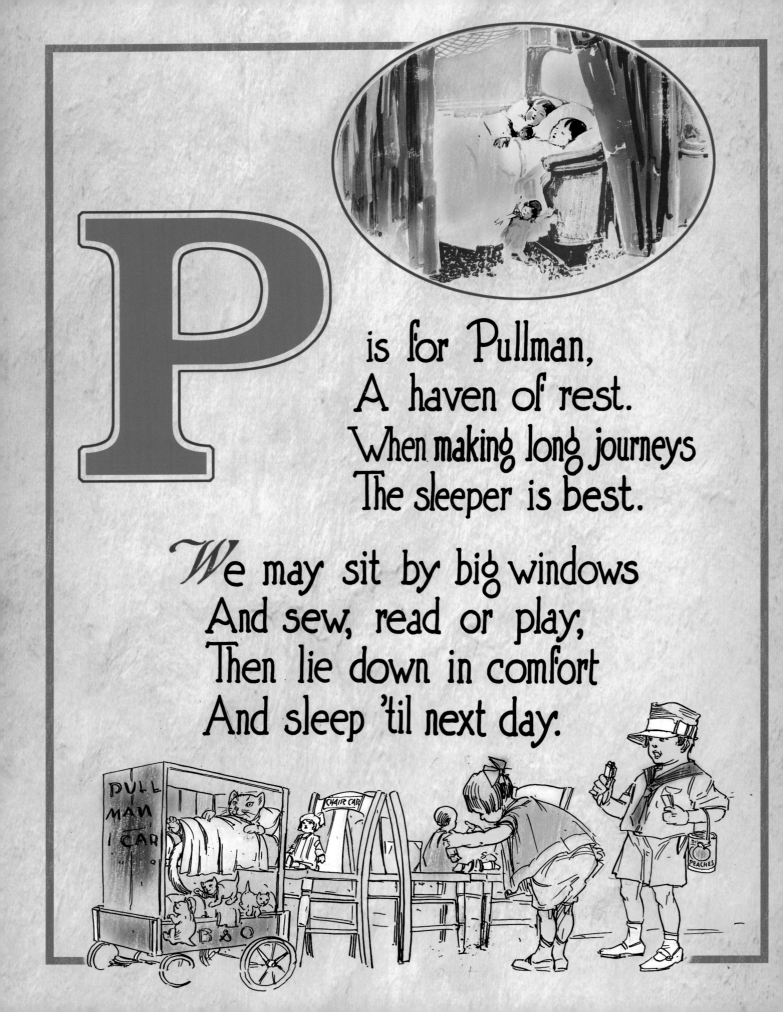

P is for Pullman,
A haven of rest.
When making long journeys
The sleeper is best.

We may sit by big windows
And sew, read or play,
Then lie down in comfort
And sleep 'til next day.

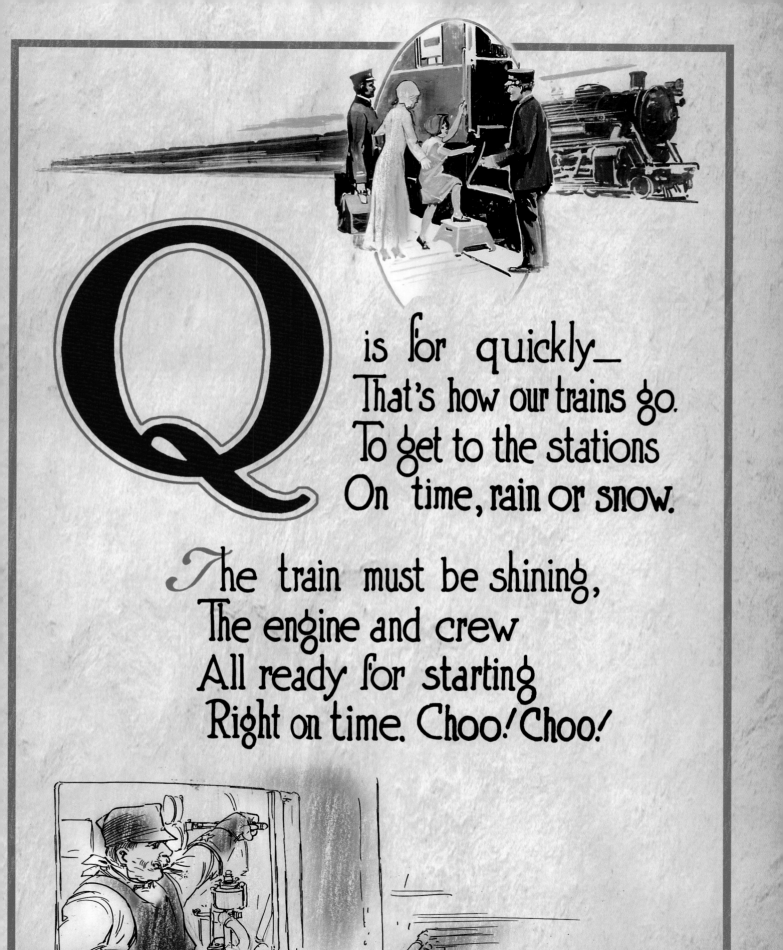

Q is for quickly—
That's how our trains go.
To get to the stations
On time, rain or snow.

The train must be shining,
The engine and crew
All ready for starting
Right on time. Choo! Choo!

R is for rivers,
All rippling and gay,
We watch them from our
Train windows each day.

They make lovely pictures
For children like me___
As I ride on the train
They run to the sea.

S is for safety,
For service and shop,
For savings and semaphore,
Slow-up and stop.

But safety is first,
Above everything—
That's why whistles blow
And engine bells ring

T

is for towers
  Where operators stay
To see that the train
  Goes just the right way.

While you're soundly sleeping
They're watching up there
And awaiting the orders
They handle with care.

U is for useful,
And you'll surely find
The Baltimore and Ohio's
A road of that kind.

Useful for pleasure,
For business or fun;
A friendlier railroad
There never was one.

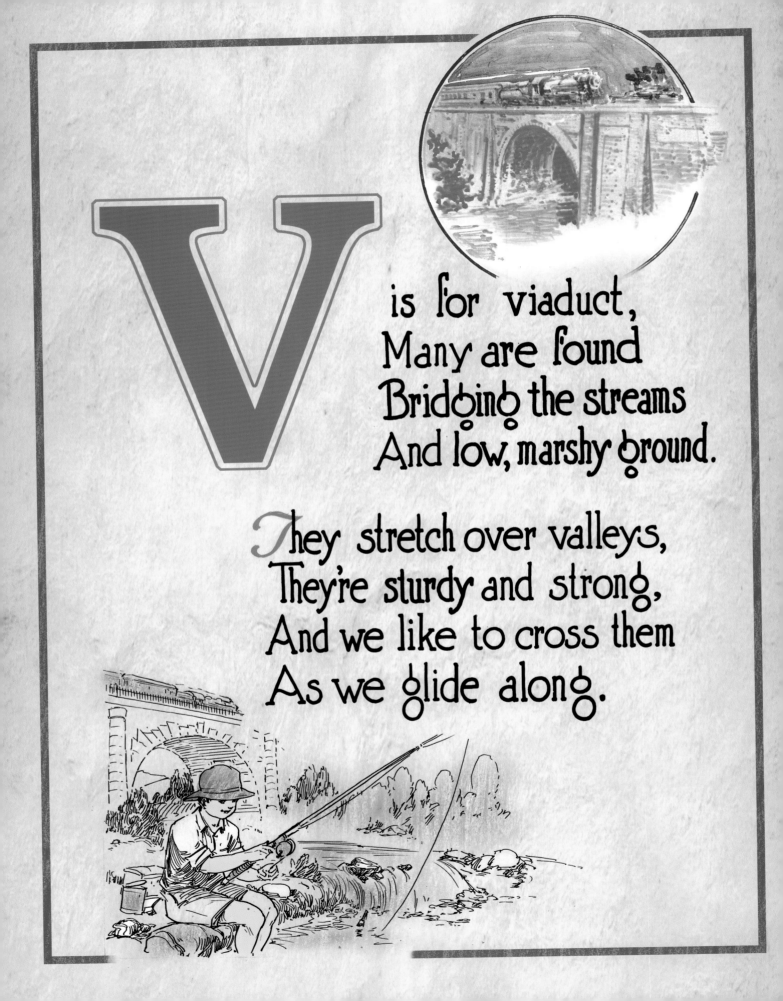

V is for viaduct,
Many are found
Bridging the streams
And low, marshy ground.

They stretch over valleys,
They're sturdy and strong,
And we like to cross them
As we glide along.

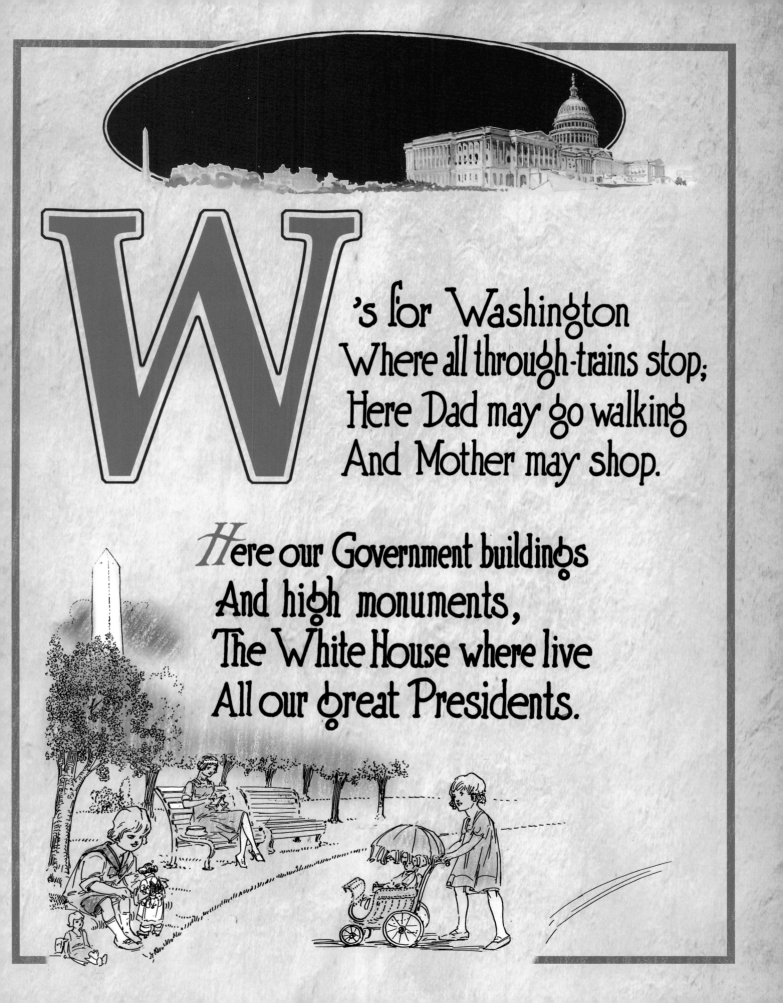

W

's for Washington
Where all through-trains stop;
Here Dad may go walking
And Mother may shop.

Here our Government buildings
And high monuments,
The White House where live
All our great Presidents.

X marks the spot
All experts agree,
Stop, look, listen,
As basic as 1-2-3.

Expect to wait before you cross
Lest one train is hiding another.
Set a good example, obey the sign,
And you will please your mother.

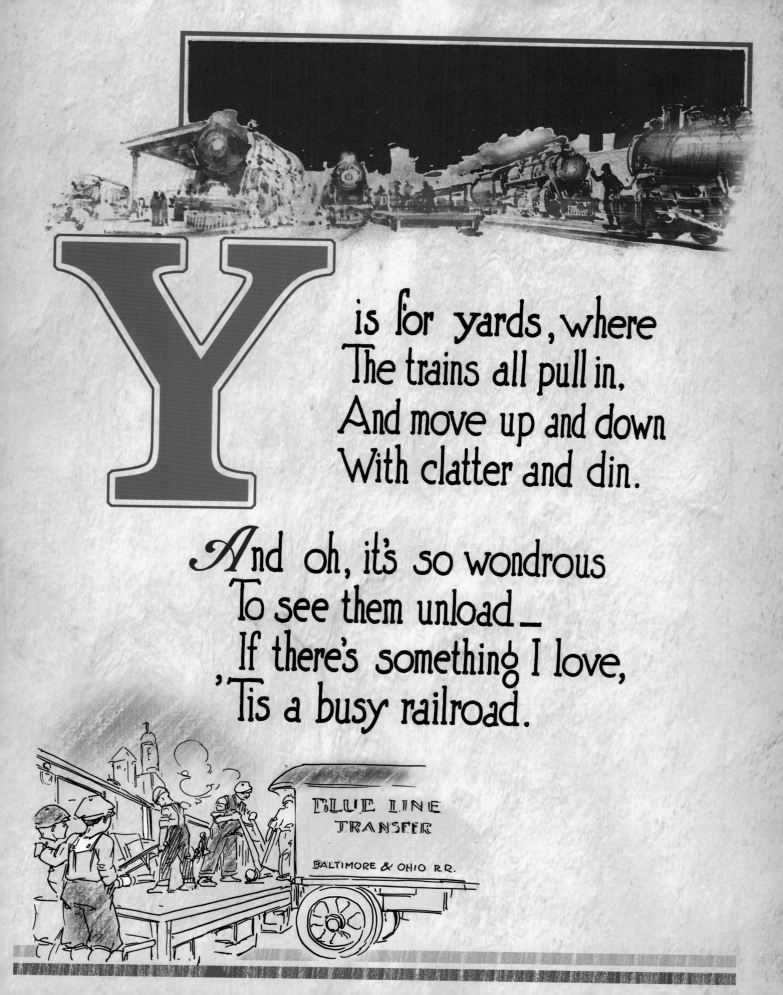

Y is for yards, where
The trains all pull in,
And move up and down
With clatter and din.

And oh, it's so wondrous
To see them unload —
If there's something I love,
'Tis a busy railroad.

BLUE LINE
TRANSFER

BALTIMORE & OHIO R.R.

Z is for zero,
Cold weather, oh, ho!
But B&O coaches
Are cosy, you know.

In summer they're cool,
In winter they're warm,
No matter the weather,
In sunshine or storm.

AFTERWORD

In the course of cataloging and organizing of the Hays T. Watkins Research Library at the Baltimore & Ohio Railroad Museum, important discoveries have been made. The Museum's archive and library consists of one of the earliest and most important documentary and photographic collections of American railroad history in the world. In addition, the collections contain an extensive commercial and fine art collection. Thousands of linear feet of material inherited from the Baltimore & Ohio Railroad, Chesapeake & Ohio Railway, the Western Maryland Railway, and hundreds of smaller railroads either acquired or subsidiaries of the B&O, will perpetuate this journey of discovery for years to come.

The ABC Choo Choo Book was discovered in mid-2004. Its superb quality and educational value was immediately recognized by our Museum curators, archivists and educators. This work was intended for publication by the Railroad's Public Relations Department in 1931, but was never printed. Two hundred thousand copies were slated for the book's first edition. They were to be distributed on board the B&O's premier passenger trains as both a customer amenity and a marketing tool. Unfortunately, the economic realities of administering a depression-era industry presumably derailed the project.

The book was written by Aunt Mary, a pen name taken by Margaret Talbott Stevens. Stevens joined the B&O in 1915 as a clerk in the Car Service Department. She was a former elementary school teacher from Anne Arundel County, Maryland. Three years later she was promoted to Chief File Clerk, and she began writing poetry, humor and technical articles for the B&O Magazine - an employee publication of the Railroad. By 1920 her sobriquet, Aunt Mary, was well established, and she became the Associate Editor of the Magazine. During her career with the B&O she was selected to represent the company on a State Department delegation to France. Following World War I, she was received by President Warren Harding at the White House, and wrote many of the scripts for the B&O's 1927 centenary celebration, The Fair of the Iron Horse. Following World War II, Ms. Stevens was promoted to Research Librarian for the Railroad and reported directly to the Office of the President. In that final role she was largely responsible for assembling much of the historical materials that have been preserved in the Hays T. Watkins Research Library at the Baltimore & Ohio Railroad Museum.

AFTERWORD

In the course of cataloging and organizing of the Hays T. Watkins Research Library at the Baltimore & Ohio Railroad Museum, important discoveries have been made. The Museum's archive and library consists of one of the earliest and most important documentary and photographic collections of American railroad history in the world. In addition, the collections contain an extensive commercial and fine art collection. Thousands of linear feet of material inherited from the Baltimore & Ohio Railroad, Chesapeake & Ohio Railway, the Western Maryland Railway, and hundreds of smaller railroads either acquired or subsidiaries of the B&O, will perpetuate this journey of discovery for years to come.

The ABC Choo Choo Book was discovered in mid-2004. Its superb quality and educational value was immediately recognized by our Museum curators, archivists and educators. This work was intended for publication by the Railroad's Public Relations Department in 1931, but was never printed. Two hundred thousand copies were slated for the book's first edition. They were to be distributed on board the B&O's premier passenger trains as both a customer amenity and a marketing tool. Unfortunately, the economic realities of administering a depression-era industry presumably derailed the project.

The book was written by Aunt Mary, a pen name taken by Margaret Talbott Stevens. Stevens joined the B&O in 1915 as a clerk in the Car Service Department. She was a former elementary school teacher from Anne Arundel County, Maryland. Three years later she was promoted to Chief File Clerk, and she began writing poetry, humor and technical articles for the B&O Magazine - an employee publication of the Railroad. By 1920 her sobriquet, Aunt Mary, was well established, and she became the Associate Editor of the Magazine. During her career with the B&O she was selected to represent the company on a State Department delegation to France. Following World War I, she was received by President Warren Harding at the White House, and wrote many of the scripts for the B&O's 1927 centenary celebration, The Fair of the Iron Horse. Following World War II, Ms. Stevens was promoted to Research Librarian for the Railroad and reported directly to the Office of the President. In that final role she was largely responsible for assembling much of the historical materials that have been preserved in the Hays T. Watkins Research Library at the Baltimore & Ohio Railroad Museum.

Her partner on the project was Charles H. Dickinson, Jr., the book's artist portrayed as Uncle Dick. Dickinson was, apparently, trained as a bookkeeper but pursued a career as a commercial artist early in the 20th century. A former artist for the Washington Post, he executed a series of oil paintings titled "Makers of the Railroad" for the exhibitions at the B&O's Fair of the Iron Horse in 1927. This series depicted various B&O workers plying their trades such as engineers, interlocking tower operators, and chemists. Many of his original oil paintings remain in the Museum's collections today. He also completed commercial art projects for the B&O used in advertising materials and a number of covers for the B&O Magazine.

H. Irving Martin (Uncle Martin) is credited with the concept for the ABC Choo Choo Book and gave the project life. His career with the B&O spanned 50 years in the Relief Department (a B&O Railroad employee protection and benefits department), and he was a common contributor to the B&O Magazine. An avid reader and scholar, he acted as a "correspondent" for the Magazine over the course of his career and contributed the major part of his personal library to the Railroad--now also part of the Museum's rare book collection.

Finally, the book is dedicated to "The Grandchildren of Daniel Willard." President of the B&O Railroad from 1910 to 1941, he led the company through World War I and the Great Depression. A staunch motivator and protector of his employees, he was always keenly concerned for their welfare. Beloved by all, he earned the sobriquet "Uncle Dan." Advisor to Presidents and renowned for his internationally-significant contributions to the railroad industry, the dedication of this little children's book is symbolic of the respect that he earned from all who worked for him and with him.

The art is timeless, and the lessons of this historic railroad story are still taught in the Museum's programs today. We are proud to offer our visitors the first publication of this historic work since its completion in 1931.

Courtney B. Wilson
Executive Director
Baltimore & Ohio Railroad Museum
March 30, 2005